# Ranking *the* Wishes

Other Books by Carl Dennis

*A House of My Own*
*Climbing Down*
*Signs and Wonders*
*The Near World*
*The Outskirts of Troy*
*Meetings with Time*

# Ranking *the* Wishes

## Carl Dennis

*Penguin Poets*

PENGUIN BOOKS
Published by the Penguin Group
Penguin Books USA Inc., 375 Hudson Street, New York, New York 10014, U.S.A.
Penguin Books Ltd, 27 Wrights Lane, London W8 5TZ, England
Penguin Books Australia Ltd, Ringwood, Victoria, Australia
Penguin Books Canada Ltd, 10 Alcorn Avenue, Toronto, Ontario, Canada M4V 3B2
Penguin Books (N.Z.) Ltd, 182–190 Wairau Road, Auckland 10, New Zealand

Penguin Books Ltd, Registered Offices:
Harmondsworth, Middlesex, England

*First published in Penguin Books 1997*

10  9  8  7  6  5  4  3  2  1

Copyright © Carl Dennis, 1997
All rights reserved

*Page vii constitutes an extension of this copyright page.*

LIBRARY OF CONGRESS CATALOGING IN PUBLICATION DATA
Dennis, Carl.
    Ranking the wishes : poems / by Carl Dennis.
        p.  cm.
    ISBN 0 14 058.779 9 (pbk.)
    I. Title.
    PS3554.E535R3      1997
    811'.54—dc21      96-44352

Printed in the United States of America
Set in Sabon
Designed by Sabrina Bowers

*For Alan Feldman*

# Acknowledgments

Thanks are due to the editors of the following magazines, in which some of the poems first appeared: *Agni* ("All I've Wanted"); *American Poetry Review* ("Days of Heaven," "The Line," "Night Drive," "Pendulum," "Sarit Narai," "Say It," and "Time Zones"); *Atlantic Monthly* ("Bivouac Near Trenton"); *Fifty Eight* ("Land and Sea" and "Parley"); *The Kenyon Review* ("Seven Days" and "Two or Three Wishes"); *Kiosk* ("The Canvasser Knocks"); *The Nation* ("Fall"); *The New Republic* ("Consolation" and "Grace"); *The Paris Review* ("The Great Day" and "Integer"); *Ploughshares* ("Distinctions" and "Writing at Night"); *Poetry* ("As If," "Holy Brethren," "Loss," "Still Life," and "To Reason"); *Prairie Schooner* ("Cedar Point," "Swindle," and "To the Soul"); *Salmagundi* ("The Pancake Hour"); *Third Coast* ("Gifts" and "Genres"); and *The Virginia Quarterly Review* ("Starry Night" and "Your City").

"Tune-Up" was originally published in *Poems for a Small Planet: Contemporary Nature Poetry*, Robert Pack and Jay Parini, eds., University Press of New England, 1993.

Finally, the author wishes to thank the friends who offered indispensable criticism of this manuscript: Charles Altieri, Thomas Centolella, Stephen Dobyns, Alan Feldman, and Martin Pops.

# Contents

# Ranking the Wishes

# Fall

The way the maples outside my window
Drop their leaves not one by one,
Like houseplants, but all together
In a shower of red and yellow, leads the unwary
To suppose them a message about renewal,
To forget the colors have always been there
Waiting beneath the green for the shorter days
When the green stops flowing.
To read the change as a promise
Of late work outshining early
Is to be lured by glitter into disappointment.
And if a lucky few of the many observers
Excited by the leaves to a final effort
Somehow succeed, their lives ever afterward
Seem veiled by a mist of fiction,
However undeniable their accomplishments. Unreal
Like the lives of those early settlers,
Pious sectarians, who persuaded themselves
That New England was all theirs,
Deeded to them in a holy covenant,
A delusion that bestowed great confidence,
Great power. Of course I'm glad they came.
Otherwise I wouldn't be sitting here
Looking out the window at the fiery maples,
Telling myself again and again it's foolish
To believe their leaves are letters
Sent from the capital to the provinces
With news of a brightness as yet unseen
Waiting in the dark for a sign from me.

# Cedar Point

The woman who cooked her heart out at Cedar Point
High in the Adirondacks wouldn't have minded so much
When nobody came to the kitchen to praise her work
If she'd believed her work recorded by a watchful heaven.
Sad that a faith like that was denied her,
That she lived in a skeptical, fretful era
Not rich in serious witnesses. The guests at Cedar Point,
Lacking either the taste required or the concentration,
Bolted dessert in their rush to get back to the lake
For an evening sail or ramble or bingo game.
In an age of faith the joy of achievement
Would have been enough, and she needn't have dreamed
Of consuming in vengeance a feast intended for ninety
All by herself while the guests ate crackers.
Just herself at the table with her one friend, Cindy,
The young, willowy waitress who never smiled,
Who was bullied all day by the manager
With his no-nonsense lantern jaw and raspy voice.
In an age of faith Cindy might have believed
Her sorrow recorded in a heavenly ledger,
But in the age she lived in only the helpless cook
Looked on with concern and maybe the gentle boy
At table seven, who asked her questions.
As for the faith of the boy, he could imagine a potion
That Cindy's stepmother, desperate for youth,
Received for abandoning Cindy to the manager,
But not a potion to make a boy of eleven
A knight by summer's end, a deliverer.
And now, forty years later, when the cook
Has long since sweated her last in the thankless kitchen,
The whole burden of witnessing falls on him.

Even the woman that Cindy's become
Might not remember, sixty years old at least
If still alive, retired to Florida for all he knows,
Carting her grandchildren to baseball practice
While her husband, sporty in cleats and cap,
Tees off with his chums. No witness left
But a man who admits he has no answers
As he asks how to save Cindy the Beautiful
Still stranded in her attic room,
Ironing the uniform of her prison
Or lugging the heavy trays
From the steamy kitchen without a smile,
Not expecting her luck to change.

# Time Zones

For me this moment on the bench in Frontier Park,
2:35 P.M., July 27th, marks the conclusion
Of my recordable history and the beginning
Of the many possible histories I can choose from.
But for the immortal angel supposed to guide me,
Sitting invisible on the bench across from mine,
This moment's a scene in a play he knows by heart,
Marking the well-worn spot where I lose my way
Or finally turn from the field of fading pleasures
Up the stone path that leads to enlightenment.
No suspense for the angel. He knows what's coming.
And no regret. However well I do or badly
He believes the show must go on
Whether the audience grows sad or happy.
Here on this bench, I think I'm ready
For any advice the angel is ready to give me,
But all I hear are the sounds of children
Playing in the sandbox, with mothers and fathers
Calling them to play gently. In the angel's mind
This scene foreshadows a scene of recognition
When I look from a window during my final illness
At a park playground like this and remember this moment
And draw a connection. But will the name I give it
Be similar to the name the angel gives?
And if there's a difference, how much will it matter?
These are questions the angel will try
To help me with, but with no more success
Than he seems to be having now. Is he still hopeful?
Maybe he figures there's not much point
In making an effort if he knows the end already,
Including all the sentences I'll come up with

And the meaning I'll choose to give them.
Still for the angel it can't be easy to watch me
Waiting all afternoon on a bench in the park
As if all I needed to get things right
Was a little more information.

# Loss

Just because your cousins perjured themselves
On the stand to steal the house you inherited
And have settled in, and are filling the rooms
With furniture your aunt would have hated,
Doesn't mean they're getting away with it.

Just because their lights will now burn late
In the house you love, and the sound of their dancing
Will be heard in the street, their drums and trumpets
At birthday parties, graduations, and weddings,
Doesn't mean they're not paying the penalty,
Living lesser lives than they might have lived,
Possessing lesser amounts of comeliness.

And if they're not aware of the loss,
Couldn't that show how shrunken their spirits are,
How you wouldn't want to be them as they fall asleep
At the end of a day they regard as perfect?

Of course it's hard not to wish them ill,
A pain that even their thicker souls can feel.
But that won't widen your cramped apartment.
That won't give you the spacious, airy life you admire
With windows opening out on the horizon.

Pity them if you can't forget them.
And if that's too hard for now, pity the house.
Think how it's losing out on the care
You'd have bestowed on it, on the loyalty
You'd have shown to its style and character,

Not to your fancy, a distinction too fine
For the new owners to handle.

Be like those angels said to enjoy the earth
As a summer retreat before man entered the picture,
Staggering under his sack of boundary stones.
They didn't mutter curses as they fastened their wings
And rose in widening farewell circles.
They grieved for the garden growing smaller below them,
Soon to exist only as a story
That every day grows harder to believe.

# Days of Heaven

That was a great compliment the Greeks paid to human life
When they imagined their gods living as humans do,
With the same pleasure in love and feasting,
Headstrong as we are, turbulent, quick to anger,
Slow to forgive. Just like us, only immortal.
And now that those gods have proven mortal too
And heaven and earth can't be divided,
Every death means a divine occasion
Has been taken from us, a divine perspective,
Though the loss gets only a line or two in the news.
Hard to believe the headlines this morning
That a banker on Mt. Olympus has been pilfering,
That a builder has been guilty of shoddy construction
On a bridge that spans a river in heaven,
Cutting corners to squirrel away his fortune
For a better day, when the great day has already come.
For news that heartens we must turn to the classifieds.
Here in what's left of heaven it's right to advertise
For a soul mate. It's right to look for a job
That lets us incarnate spirit more fully
And leave something behind that time is kinder to
Than the flesh of gods. Lucky there's work.
Lucky the streets of heaven are in need of repair.
Paint is peeling from the dream-house trim.
Holy rainwater backs up in leaf-clogged gutters
Till the ceiling sags and tiles need regrouting.
And look at the list of practical items for sale—
Used snowblowers, croquet sets, chainlink fencing.
And what about a wooden canoe with two paddles.
Why don't we make time for a turn before sundown?
Out on the broad lake a breeze will find us

That's wafted around the planet to cool our divinity.
The clouds will hover above us in a giant halo
As we watch our brother, the sun, descend,
His gentle face turned towards us, his godly expression
Undarkened by accusation or disappointment
Or the thought of something he's left undone.

# To Reason

I hope I never speak ill of you,
Dependable homely friend who prods me gently
To turn to the hour that's now arriving,
Not to the hour I let slip by
Twenty years back. No way now, you say,
To welcome a friend I failed to welcome
When she returned to town in sorrow,
Fresh from her discovery that the man
Who seemed to outshine all the others
Could also cast the densest shade.

You're right to label it magical thinking
When I say to a phantom what I never said
To flesh and blood, as if the words, repeated enough,
Could somehow work their way back to an old page
And nudge the silence aside and settle in, a delusion
Not appropriate for a man no longer young
At the end of a century where many nations
Have set many things in motion they can't call back
Though the vote for reversal is unanimous.

I'm glad you ask, clear-sighted Reason,
Before what audience, if my speech can't reach her ears,
I imagine myself performing. Who is it
I want to convince I'd do things differently
This time around if the chance were offered.
You're right to say that half an hour a day is enough
For these gods or angels to get the point
If they're ever going to get it, which is doubtful.
Right again that if part of myself
After all my efforts still needs convincing

I should leave that dullard behind
With the empty dream of wholeness and move on.

I should move along the road that is not the road
I'd be moving along had I said what I didn't say
To someone who might have been ready to listen,
But a road as good, you assure me, Reason,
One that might lead to a life I can be proud of
So the man I might have been can't pity me.

Thanks for contending I can solve the problems
He may have wanted to solve but hadn't the time for,
Preoccupied as he was with another life,
The one I too might be caught up in
Had I heard the words you now speak clearly
Just as clearly long ago.

# Gifts

Though her feelings for the man across town
Who writes her weekly are a tiny fraction
Of his feelings for her, and will always be,
She doesn't return his letters unopened.
It may do him good to believe she scans them
All year long, even, as now, at tax time,
A bookkeeper's busiest season, her weeknights
Commandeered by the office and many weekends.

Half an hour with his thoughts on Sunday
Hasn't hurt her so far, or stowing them in a shoe box.
And if April's hard for her, it's harder for him
In his landscape business. His customers want new lawns.
Lights are flashing on his phone when he gets home,
His back aching, his clothes crusted. But the calls
Must wait till he's done with a paragraph
For her eyes only on his luck with organic mixes.

Now his news may bore her, granted, but on gray days
When those who matter most don't seem to value
Her high regard as she'd like them to,
It does her good to think of her photograph
Commanding the messy desk of a practical man
With taste and talent who feels compelled
To practice the lonely art of non-reciprocity,
An art that civilization requires for the virtues
Of graciousness and gratitude to reach full flower.

Yes, her busy schedule keeps her from visiting
The shelf in her heart set aside for him
As much as she'd like, but for all he knows

She may be thinking of him this very minute.
That's reason enough for the sudden rush of joy
She imagines descending on him out of nowhere
As he makes a note to himself about grub control
Or a lawn to be roto-tilled tomorrow and seeded.

Most days she may see herself as dodging her way
Through a maze of traffic, a thin woman in a red raincoat
Rushing so as not to be late for her next appointment.
Now and then he helps her think of herself
As one of those old churches that welcomed the work
Of every sculptor who made an effort, who took pains.

Some statues were given a niche in the entry arch
Obvious to all visitors, and some a perch high up
Visible to any monk in the choir
Willing to crane his neck or to any angel
Pausing among the rafters to rest
Before darting away on another mission.

# Pendulum

If I sleep through the moment just before dawn
When the pendulum of the day reaches the top
Of its swing and pauses, I can catch the other pause
At dusk, when the street outside the window
Appears suspended, lifted from its surroundings
And held motionless, and I'm able to ask
Why these particular houses have been selected
To compose my world, and why now,
When my soul feels fluid,
Kin to everyone who has ever lived here
From the time of the earliest settler till today.
A puff of wind in the snowball bush at the curb.
A puff over the waist-high, shaggy grass
Rolling away from the farmhouse in all directions
As a woman steps out on the porch in dusky light
To ring the bell. Just as she reaches up
To summon her son and husband from the barn
The pendulum of the day reaches its pausing point
And her gaze grows tentative and confused.
What is this place to her, this endless prairie,
This wilderness fit for a soul that asks to be lonely
Under a boundless sky, which she never asked for
Or only in one of her many moods.
Hasn't she dreamed for two nights running
Of a woman walking home from the opera
Through the streets of Paris, humming a theme?
Two women playing their parts in separate dramas
Or one woman divided. That's the issue for her
As she watches the grass from the porch
Billow and bend while time's suspended.
The wind crosses the prairie, skirts the woods,

And shakes the snowball bush at the curb
Across from the self-same row of houses,
Motionless and unyielding, blocking my vista.
And then her hand tightens on the rope
And the pendulum, poised, starts on its downswing
As the bell sounds, and the day parts
Soundlessly like the grass to let us in.

# Parley

Could be everyone is a country with a separate climate,
With its own courtrooms, merchant marine, and prophets.
And every conversation is a meeting of ambassadors
In a mountainous no-man's land where a mob of echoes
Makes every speech sound equally foreign.

Could be it doesn't pay the runner in training again
For his annual one-man marathon around the pond
To try explaining why he has to run.
It doesn't pay the man in line at the flower stall
To try convincing us his Juliet is the goddess
He knows she is. Doesn't pay the lover of wisdom,
Reading upstairs at his desk all day,
To descend to the street at dusk with a proof
His mode of ignorance is deeper and larger.

How then explain the sight of four people in a restaurant
Laughing together over a story, four friends
Who've grown so tired by dessert of mocking the president
They construct another president out of airy nothing.
And what about after dinner when two of the four
Walk home in twilight through the public garden,
Though one contends the bush up ahead in shadows
Looks like a wolf, and the other like a bear.

Two false alarms, they agree, from the limbic system
That helped to keep the species watchful,
The pioneers on the guard,
Till cities arose with gardens like this
Where people like them can ramble in safety
Till night comes on and the watchmen leave.

❋

It's a good place for them to discuss the fears
That till now were hidden. One to admit
He's worried he'll say too much
If he doesn't edit his revelations.
One to lament she can't come up with the words
That sound as open and trusting
After they're spoken as they do before.

# Seven Days

No problem making sense of the week
Once I convince myself that each day
Is meant to follow the one before
Or not to follow, whichever it chooses.
One day for me to be the rabbi upstairs
Mapping the twelve degrees of righteousness.
One day to put the first degree into practice,
Figuring how to allow the gleaners
To gather sheaves in my field after the harvest
When I have no field, just a yard in town.
And then a sunny day for making my yard
A kingdom of flowers to delight the eye.
And a rainy day for sketching the yellow flower
Adorning the hair of the goddess Luna
As she rows her boat through a black sky.
And then a day to be sad this image of fulfillment
Would be just as strange to the rabbi
As his love of commandments would be to her,
However many letters I carried between them.
And a day to be happy I can talk to one
And then the other, and agree with both,
Undaunted by contradiction and inconsistency.
And then one day of rest from wondering
If I'm to bless them as my own creation
Or if they're to bless me as their restless child.

# Sarit Narai

Now that the light holds on after supper,
Why not walk west to the end of Ferry Street
And linger where the ferries used to dock
Before the bridge spanned the Niagara.
Why not enlarge the thin verge of the moment
With the Sunday crowd on deck fifty years ago
Riding to Fort Erie and back just for the fun of it.
The wind from the lake ruffles their hair
As the low sun glances along the water.
Just as they left their rooms to join the flow
So you can go back to them for a moment
And lead them forward into the present
Where the gulls are gliding, swinging beneath the bridge
In figures that blur as you watch, and disappear.
And why not call up the boys you used to see here
Playing on the boulders in the bridge's shadow
Before the fence was put up to stop them.
If one of them lost his footing, his chances were slim,
The push in the channel too hard and heavy,
The water of Erie beginning its headlong, brainless rush
To join the Ontario, as if an extra minute mattered.
Remember the evening you found a crowd here
Waiting beside an ambulance with its motor running
And a squad car where a woman sat in back
Head in her hands? Dark-haired. Next morning
Leafing through the local news, you found the story—
Woman from Thailand, three years in the States,
Loses her son, eleven, to the Niagara.
Let yourself go, if you want to enlarge the moment,
And imagine what might have happened if the boy,
Sarit Narai, had been fished from the river in time.

Try to think of him as your son's best friend
At Niagara school, where friends were scarce,
Quieting a wildness you could never manage,
The mild manners of Asia persuasive by mere example.
And what if your daughter admires him even more
And comes to choose him for her life's companion,
Not the drab complainer she ended up with.
The world turned left that day on the forking path
But the path on the right still runs beside it
Though never touching. A bountiful Buddha smile
As he explains to your granddaughters and grandsons
How to climb the eightfold path to freedom
As gulls like these swoop over the gray stones
And the ferries steam back and forth if you let them.
Freely the crowd on deck empties its mind of thought
And welcomes sensation, the sun and wind.
And then the riders waken to see the skyline of home
Beckoning from a distance as if it missed them,
So they're ready to take up their lives again
As the ship pulls in where now a line of cars
Waits in the twilight to pay the bridge toll
Not thirty yards from the spot where the ambulance waited
And the woman cried in the back seat of the car.
After an hour the crowd moved off, dissolving to families,
To couples musing on twilight pastimes.
For a moment, though, each may have hesitated
To change the subject and appear small-souled.
The mist of sorrow already thinning and fading
That would have remained if they'd lived in Eden,
The one kingdom where the sorrows of others
Feel like our own. When Buddha neared Nirvana,

One story goes, he looked back on us as we drowned
In the sea of endless craving, and was filled with pity,
And chose to postpone his bliss till all were saved.
But how can a climb from the world be managed here
When the crowd on the ferry wants the sunset to linger,
And the mother would sell her soul to get her son back,
And the boy still struggles to grab the slippery rock
And pull himself up, his friends all helping
So he can grow old among them. An old man
Looking back on his deeds of kindness. Now the few
Who met him and the many who never did but might have
Feel the phantom gap he would have filled
But are ignorant of its cause and blame their wives,
Their husbands, their children, their towns and jobs,
And hunt around for new gospels, new philosophies.
If you see them this evening pacing along the bank
Where once the ferries docked and the Sunday riders
Lost themselves awhile in the sway and shimmer,
Pity their restlessness. There must be a way
To step forward and name the one they miss,
Sarit Narai, in a tone so resonant
It holds them a moment beyond loss and longing.

# Holy Brethren

If I don't believe the doctrine of my neighbor's church,
The church of the Holy Brethren, that we're sinners all
And need to repent each night and ask forgiveness,
I don't believe it's foolish.
Some metaphor of the truth could be hidden there,
A crust from a loaf baked long ago
And broken and scattered among the seekers.

And if his church nurtures his many virtues,
I'm glad he belongs, my generous neighbor,
First to help when my basement's flooded,
Last to leave the soup kitchen Saturday night
When others have gone dancing.

May the fund drive he's heading go well this year
So the clapboard walls of the meeting hall
In the low-rent district can be repainted,
Its burden of debt lifted to lift his spirits.
May he feel less driven to hunt around
For an incarnation that seems more tangible,
More potent than the one his church is built on.

It hurts me to see how he's planted in front of his house
A thirty-foot, silvery flagpole with a ten-foot flag.
I wish its flapping sounded like the soft voices of sinners
Who know that flesh is a match for spirit,
Not like the voice of the justified, who can do no wrong.

Does he guess the snap and pop keep me from sleeping?
If he does, I should try not to be offended.
He has reason to be angry he's growing old

With no sign that the side he's on
Can win a battle once in a while
As his country does, an actual battle
Praised in the papers and honored with feasting.

Why not one day when his enemies look like enemies,
Not like one of his own moods writ large?
One day when they're all plowed under as weeds
And don't appear next morning higher than the corn.

# Swindle

Now I know why the salesman in the used-car lot
Gave me a box of cigars when I signed the papers.
Still, for a couple of weeks each month
It starts in the morning and runs all right.
And it doesn't shimmy if I stay near thirty.
A good speed for a Sunday drive.
I can get off the freeway and enjoy the scenery.
I can linger at fruit stands or nap in a field.

Bumpy as its ride is,
It still handles more easily
Than the noiseless triumph of engineering
Advertised as my life.
At least I can turn my car around in the rain
When the gravel road looks doubtful.
At least the wheel doesn't seize up when I realize
I left my favorite book at the doughnut diner.

No wheel at all for turning around
And swinging back for the friend
I promised to bring along
But forgot when I got distracted.

I got distracted a while ago,
But now I'm eager to go back.
And the rattletrap I drive, that joke of vandals,
Is ready to get me there
And let me explain myself and ask for pardon.

It's only life that's the problem,
Life, the famous intricate miracle

That daily converts a crowd of unbelievers.
So many options and still it can't be maneuvered
To take me in any direction except one.
Only one, hour after hour.
Only forward.

# Say It

Say it wasn't your eloquence, as you supposed,
That won your wife's affections but the odd,
Congenital squeak in your voice that reminded her
Of her dad's voice, which was squeakier.
Say you didn't earn her as Jacob earned Rachel,
Toiling seven years, and seven more,
When you marked on your sample ballot at the polling place
The same losers she planned to vote for,
When you spoke of the many unfriendly porch steps
You'd climbed on weekends to canvass for true reform,
When you detailed the doors slammed in your face
Just as you opened your argument for higher taxes.
Why should it make you sad to leave the club
Of the self-made, where the meetings drone on
As each of the members lists his accomplishments?
Why not prefer the club of the lucky, the blessed,
Where you can muse in your garden beside the lilacs
Already tall and fragrant when you moved in?
Once it seemed important that you cleared the yard
By hand from a tangle of underbrush,
That you bricked the path and cleaned the fountain.
Let it now be more relevant to your pleasure
To muse on the box of miniature garden tools
Your father gave you fifty years back,
The ones your mother let you keep playing with
When the children next door called you to their games.
Wonder how she managed to resist her fear
You'd be a loner, where she got the faith
A friend was included among the gifts
Time was planning to send your way.

# Night Drive

It's a black mark next to the name of our species
When people are forced to confide their troubles to trees
Or rivers, to the sun or moon. That's why I've given
So much of my free time to the art of listening,
Why I've practiced the exercises for focusing my attention,
For ridding my face of the squint of judgment.
It's no accident that at parties a line forms
Beside my chair, a line of strangers
Eager to unburden themselves to a quiet man
Who never consults his watch as they linger over details.
That's why that gray-haired woman told me this evening
How her husband caught miner's fever, a disease of the brain
That made him prefer the dank of the underworld
To the warm sunshine above and left her a widow
More than a decade before he died.
The way I kept silent encouraged her to go on,
The tilt of my head better than any medicine
Though she had to sit down when finished and catch her breath.
Then, had things gone as they should have,
She'd have thanked me and let me turn to the next,
Not asked me to fetch her bottle of blood-pressure pills
From a desk in her house back in the canyon
Seven miles from town, as if my talent
Were driving and fetching, not listening.
"You can't miss it," she said. "Don't mind the dog
Or the shouting upstairs from Uncle Igor."
Seven miles on a swampy road
Where the houses are badly lit and the numbers missing.
I'd never have agreed if she hadn't insisted
I was the only guest she could trust to find it
And return with her house key. Seven miles,

And by the time I get back she'll be feeling fine,
Waving a cheery good-bye to the hostess.
And the many guests I needed to hear,
Who came to the party searching for a listener,
Will be walking one by one to their cars,
Wondering if they should offer their stories
To the moon, the distant moon that offers
No heat or light to work by,
Just the sight, far off, of its yellow face.

# The Line

No denying it's hard to watch them,
The two couples who broke in line ahead of us,
Sitting now in the seats we might have chosen
Down in the orchestra, leaning forward
As if they cared about Brutus and Caesar.

If they're as confident as they seem,
Certain their pleasures take precedence over ours,
It won't occur to them that Caesar, however ambitious,
Had to work for his honors, serving the state.
These couples come from a time long gone
Before the notion of a commonwealth was conceived.
Before the concept of a line won out over a scrimmage.

To them the principle of one line for everyone
Must seem as crazy as a single shoe size.
Let each have his own line, at a separate entrance.
That's their kind of proposal—flamboyant,
Unfeasible—that lets them regard themselves
As lonely dreamers, born before their time.

Nothing so vulgar for them, if they deem the mayor
A would-be tyrant, as collecting signatures
Door to door on a recall petition. No stomach
For following Brutus as he takes his principles
Out from his trellised garden to the mess of the world
Where embodiment never escapes contamination.
They prefer a cloistered purity useful to none.

Do you suppose the fear of becoming soiled
Kept us from telling them what we thought,

Or the fear of losing our dignity in a shouting contest?
Let's hope we're as willing now to look foolish
As we were last spring on the courthouse lawn,
Making a spectacle of ourselves banging pots and pans
In sympathy with the troublemaker inside
Who'd burned the flag in a private protest.

For him it was merely the flag of Antony and Octavian,
The winners, not the beautiful flag of Brutus,
All night a target for the slings of the Empire
And at dawn still there.

# Tune-Up

Before tomorrow's drive to the woods
For a walk in the zone of eternal cycles,
I have time to watch today the gray-haired mechanic
At Hodge and Elmwood tune my sedan.
As he stands in the bay, listening to the hum,
He wipes his brow on his forearm, hands too greasy,
And I notice the tattoo I've noticed before,
Three roses with the inscription "Manila, 1950."
Tomorrow the timeless beauty of ripples
Scudding in sunlight over Miller's Pond;
Today a moment of indelible history.
No reason to think he's ashamed that once,
On shore leave, the young sailor he used to be
Considered the moment worthy of commemoration.
Maybe now he wishes other good times
Were also inscribed there, living proof,
After he lost his photos and letters, that his life
Was eventful, that he didn't dream it away
Though the years have stranded him here at Blackwell's Garage
In a city he never assumed he'd settle in.
Tomorrow I'll watch the wind send last year's leaves
Scurrying through the woods, and I'll be safe
In the smoky light from the weight of eras.
Today there's time for watching a man gaze off
A moment into the middle distance as if wondering
If he's squeezed all the joy available from days gone by.
Strange that the past, fixed as it is, seems more of a mystery
Than the future, less forthcoming, less predictable.
I know the paths I'm likely to walk tomorrow
And the hour I'm likely to walk them, rain or shine,
While here on Elmwood the man listening to my car

May wonder if whoever he was is alive this minute,
Still planning what he used to plan
As he leaned on a bridge rail and looked down
At the water rushing around the piers
And heard it churning. Many more overtones then
Than he can hear now in my motor's hum
Which simply tells him this job is finished
And he can turn to another as I drive off
Dreaming of the hum I expect tomorrow.

# The Canvasser Knocks

Sorry to pull you away from your dinner,
But to get George Wilmer's name on the ballot for mayor
I'm willing to be intrusive. Give me a minute
And I'll try to explain why you should sign my petition
Despite what you may have read in the papers.
Just because he wants a curfew on teens,
More police on the streets, and stiffer sentences
Doesn't mean he's only concerned with short-term answers.
He's got some long-range ideas about our neighborhoods—
Tenant buy-back programs and investment cooperatives—
Spelled out in the pamphlet I'd like to give you
If you think you'll find a moment before the election
To scan the particulars. As for backing the hockey rink
Over the new hall for the symphony, that's not the cold
Calculation for votes that it seems so much as a tactic
To pull more shoppers into the few stores downtown
Still trying to fight the malls.
What won his support for the downtown expressway
That sliced a corner off Delaware Park
Wasn't a cheque from the highway lobby.
A cut in commuting time means extra minutes
At home with the kids. How much the family
Is under the gun in these lean times
I don't have to tell you. It bothered me too
To see the number of Wilmers on his payroll
When he was a councilman, but at least they showed,
Unlike the relatives of the other candidates.
At least they punched in and pushed their papers.
Yes, he's got an arrogant streak. Better that
Than the sweet talk we get from our mayor now.
Do good manners mean so much?

Have it your way. I don't begrudge a man like Wilmer
My one free evening this week, talking to people
Like you, too stubborn to listen.
You tell me if you see a man on horseback
Riding up the street with a ten-point program
To rebuild the city with stone, not clapboard.
With a fountain on every corner and an academy.
Look at how many neighbors have signed my petition.
What document are you saving your signature for?
Where is it being written? Who's writing it?
How long will it take to reach your door?

# Aunt Celia, 1961

A life without remorse, that's something
I'm willing to predict for a generous,
Brave young man like you. But as for happiness,
There you need luck, the kind I had
In meeting your Uncle Harry after I'd given up
Thinking I'd find a man to suit me.
The blind luck of visiting a cousin in Pittsburgh
In the spring of 1930, of going along
When she went to the lecture at the socialist club,
Of sitting at the back of the hall near the exit,
Of forgetting my scarf and having to run back,
Of stumbling over a chair and falling.
A fretful, impulsive girl helped to her feet by a man
Who turned out cheerful and philosophical.

It isn't gratitude that I felt then or feel now.
More a mixture of wonder, relief, and fear
When I imagine the girl I was back then
Making do with the luck most people have,
Missing the unknown rendezvous by inches,
The scarf not left behind, the meeting canceled,
The trip to Pittsburgh postponed a week
So she could be home for her mother's birthday.

People will tell you there are many good lives
Waiting for everyone, each fine in its own way.
And maybe they're right, but in my opinion
One is miles above the others.
Otherwise it wouldn't have been so clear to me
When I found it. Otherwise those who lack it
Wouldn't be able to tell so clearly it's missing

As they go on living as best they can
Without complaining. Noble lives, and beautiful,
And happy as much as doing well can make them.
But as for the happiness that can't be earned,
The kind it makes no sense for you to look for,
That's something different.

# As If

Before dawn, while you're still sleeping,
Playing the part of a dreamer whose house is an ark
Tossed about by a flood that will never subside,
Its dove doomed to return with no twig,
Your neighbor's already up, pulling his boots on,
Playing the part of a fisherman,
Gathering gear and loading his truck
And driving to the river and wading in
As if fishing is all he's ever wanted.

Three trout by the time you get up and wash
And come to breakfast served by a woman who smiles
As if you're first on her short list of wonders,
And you greet her as if she's first on yours.
Then you're off to school to fulfill your promise
To lose yourself for once in your teaching
And forget the clock facing your desk. Time to behave
As if the sun's standing still in a painted sky
And the day isn't a page in a one-page notebook
To be filled by sundown or never filled,
First the lines and then the margins,
The words jammed in till no white shows.

And while you're speaking as if everyone's listening,
A mile from school, at the city hall,
The mayor is behaving as if it matters
That the blueprints drawn up for the low-rent housing
Include the extra windows he's budgeted,
That the architects don't transfer the funds
To shutters and grates as they did last year
But understand that brightness is no extravagance.

And when lunch interrupts him, it's a business lunch
To plan the autumn parade, as if the fate of the nation
Hangs on keeping the floats of the poorer precincts
From looking skimpy and threadbare.

The strollers out on the street today
Don't have to believe all men are created equal,
All endowed by their creator with certain rights,
As long as they behave as if they do,
As if they believe the country will be better off
If more people do likewise, that acting this way
May help their fellow Americans better pursue
The happiness your housemate believes she's pursuing
Sharing her house with you, that the fisherman
Wants to believe he's found in fishing.

Now while you're thinking you can make her happy
As long as she's willing to behave as if you can
The fisherman keeps so still on his log
As he munches a biscuit that the fish
Rise to the surface to share his crumbs.
And the heron stands on the sandbank silently staring
As if it's wondering what the man is thinking,
Its gray eyes glinting like tin or glass.

# The Messenger

Those eight confused black men and women
Bussed from some home for the slow
And herded together at the gate an hour ago
For early boarding, might be interpreted,
Were I a believer, as messengers
Sent with a lesson for me as I waited becalmed
At the Oakland airport. A reproof
For brooding on the distance between the life
I've imagined for myself and the life I'm living.
Eight sentences in large type to show me by contrast
How lucky I've been, how all my regrets
Are merely the after-dinner regrets of ordering fish
At a banquet of friends instead of brisket.
And when I boarded the plane and found I was seated
Next to the guardian of the group, wasn't it tempting
To see her as hand-delivered to my address,
A black woman in purple slacks, fifty or so, and stout,
Mailed years back to arrive at the very moment
It helps me the most to hear her explain
How she's taking her charges to Disneyland.
"What a workout," she sighs, "but they like it so much
It's hard to say no. It's their favorite adventure
Next to the annual congress of gospel choirs
Scheduled this summer in Chicago.
They're counting the days."
Don't these words make her a messenger
Who's run all the way to tell me that spirit
Can show itself not only in wishing for more delight
Than the threadbare world can offer
But also in blessing its frayed particulars.
And now that I've read her message and understood,

Isn't it time for her to remove her heavy costume
And send her charges back to the prop room
And hope for an easier assignment next time?
So hard for me to believe she's stuck with this one,
To think of her at the end of this day
In her first free hour when the house is sleeping.
Is she reading brochures at the kitchen table
On early retirement, which she can't afford yet?
Or is she feeling what I couldn't feel,
Satisfied in the hope that upstairs
The sleepers are dreaming about their travels,
Good dreams that the angel of sleep,
Who has to put up with so many bad ones,
Has been waiting all evening to record.

# The Great Day

What if the great day never comes
And your life doesn't shine with vivid blossoms,
Just with the usual pale variety?
What if the best china never seems called for,
Those dishes reserved for the friends you love the most
On the day they return from their endless travels?
To use them now, for the only occasions available,
Would be to confuse the high realm with the low.
But not to use them, doesn't that seem wrong too,
To leave the best wine undrunk in the cellar
For the next owner of your house to open?
What then? Can you will yourself to see a common day
The way a saint might see it, as a gift from heaven,
Or the way it appears from the window of the hospital
On the first morning the patient feels strong enough
To edge across the room and look out?
There on the street an angel policeman
Is directing the flashing mosaic of traffic.
Or can you see the day as the dead might see it,
Not the ones who'd rather rest but those delighted
To abandon the gardens of Hell, however fragrant,
For a chance at crossing the sea again in a storm?
The day their ship, long given up for lost,
Steams into the harbor, all flags flying,
Would be a day to be toasted with rose champagne
In heirloom glasses. Down the gangway they come,
A little thinner, a little unsteady,
Eyes wide in wonder at their rare good fortune.
Can you see what they see as they look around
Or feel what their friends waiting on the dock

Must feel as they run forward?
"Let me look at you," they keep saying,
Suspending their formal speech of welcome.
"You look good. You look wonderful."

# The Pond in Winter

If few of these Sunday skaters on the pond
Consider themselves beloved by heaven,
Even fewer believe they've been rejected.
And if some would be justified to complain
Of negligent parents or ungrateful friends,
They've all decided it would be a shame
To waste a day like this in a musty courtroom,
Building an air-tight case against existence.
This is the afternoon they've been waiting for.
Those with skills aren't vying for prizes
As they flout the laws of friction and gravity.
Those with none aren't making sullen comparisons
As they flop on the ice and rise again.
And if tomorrow at work they all determine
That their lives still haven't begun in earnest,
That doesn't prove this afternoon is a fiction,
Only that they're forgetful. The dust of the week
May bury the revelations of Sabbath
But a new sermon may sweep them clean
Before the ice melts so they can seize another occasion
To skate as they're skating now. How clear it is
As they glide around and around the rim
That the circle is the figure they're suited for,
Both flesh and spirit delivered for a while
From the dream of a straight and narrow path
Up the highest hill to the longest view
That will put to shame the view they know.

# All I've Wanted

Who's to say that Mrs. Gottlieb, a woman of spirit,
Wasn't right when she told our high-school class
People get what they really want,
Right in her case, at least, and in mine.
I might have learned Greek if I'd wanted to.
The dictionary and grammar book on my shelf
Were likely symbols of a wish not deep enough
To issue in practice. I might have gone to Bali
And witnessed the fire dance that my friend described
So vividly I bought a map of the island,
Brochures on accommodations, a silk shirt for the climate.
I probably thought I'd be happier here
Doing other things, some less taxing than travel,
Some more. Could be I didn't want my second choice
For heart's companion deeply enough to make her stay.
Could be I wanted the seven years of regret that followed.
It's likely I could have explored whatever it was
That blocked the flow of feeling from heart
To tongue if I'd made the effort,
Could have dug the silt from the living stream.
I must have had other projects in mind,
Other ideas for ranking the needs of my species
According to a personal formula I can't call up now
But doubtless could if I wanted to.
I must want to keep that question open
Like the question whether I'm the laborer
Who reports for work in the vineyard at the crack of dawn
Or the one who straggles in at dusk with no excuses,
Hoping this is the place where the last are first.
I must enjoy not knowing if my walk this evening
Marked the end of a full day or a day of waiting.

I must be glad that the flock of plover
Arcing above the school in close formation
Looked set apart in their own blue world,
Not heading for any retreat we share.

# Inventory

Your father's wristwatch, tie clasp, and seal ring.
The warm sweaters your mother knit you. A few books
Culled from the many recommended by teachers
Together with the few you found yourself.
A lamp to read by, a desk for writing.
That's all you'll need from the world outside
To front on your own, at your own schedule,
The facts that Thoreau enjoins us to front,
The essential ones, whatever they are,
Buried under the sediment of opinion.
Just these few possessions, with maybe a porch in back
For summer evenings, or a small yard and lawn chair
So the natural sound of crickets enters your musing.
Then you're kin to the Indians who impressed Thoreau,
Who every seven years burned all they owned
In a ritual of renewal, a declaration of freedom
From the baggage that otherwise would drag them down.
Just these few things and maybe some gardening tools
To refresh the soul after hours of deliberation,
Hand mower, shovel, dibble, trowel,
Leaf rake and dirt rake, clippers to cut some flowers
To make things festive when friends come by
Because you're going to need some friends as well
To test your conclusions and offer encouragement,
Which means a dining table might come in handy
If not a dining room. And if the conversation
Can't be contained in an evening, an extra bed
If not a guest room, and a wine shelf in the basement
Near the box of tools for keeping things in repair,
Snub-nose and long-nose pliers, screwdriver, hammer,
Try square and pry bar, assorted nails and screws.

Every seven years a ritual fire
Unless you're certain you own only the basics
And the basics are all you'll need in emergencies
Given your talent for improvising
And the willingness of the world to bestow its gifts
Just as they're needed and wishes so constant
They require, however far from fulfillment,
Only the instruments already in your possession,
Not hard to master if you keep practicing.

# The Pancake Hour

If I'm the man mixing batter in the yellow kitchen
On this particular Wednesday morning in March,
Aren't I also the man who's watching him
With eyes that look so far in all directions
The cook is merely a fleck of froth on my viewing screen?
Can I be merely him if I've made my peace
With the eons that had to pass before his snowflake
Drifted into existence and the endless stint to come
Without him in it? Of course the thought of my ghost
No longer extant to record his absence would make me dizzy
If I weren't focusing my attention mainly on pancakes,
Mixing buckwheat flour, wheat germ, and oat bran
According to a secret recipe nobody's asked me for
Though it never fails, year after year, to delight my palate
While the fashion in coats and capitals flares and fades.

Why not be grateful for my incarnation
Here and now between the pot rack and the corked-face
Bulletin board emblazoned with postcards and photos,
Landscapes and seascapes chosen by scattered friends
In search of scattered beauties to feed their spirits.
If a few of those who wished I were with them
Were with me now, napkins under their chins,
This moment doubtless would feel more festive
Though no more enduring. Should I brood
On the fate of the beautiful banquets of Samaria
Or thank my stars for the lucky cold snap in Africa
Ten million years back that thinned the forests
And brought my ancestors down from the branches
To practice walking upright, their hands free
To lug a sack of berries back to the settlement?

A few minutes of wondering why the banked fires
Of a billion stars should lead over light years
To a shadowy creature with a spatula
Presiding alone in a kitchen like this.
And then it's time for a private ritual
Directed to the genial goddess of immortal pancakes.
It's hard to see what her blessing can do for me
Or how my mortal service promotes her mission.
Still it seems right to wash the berries
As I watch the batter brown in the griddle.
Right to warm the syrup, pure grade-A maple.

# To the Soul

You can come with us if you like
If you promise not to wander away from our picnic,
Turning your back on our ritual lemonade
And two flavors of soda, hers and mine.
No lonely brooding that seems to imply
We're the reason your thoughts come slowly,
Not all at once, as they do for angels.

I used to think of you as far above me,
The pilot high in the pilot house of the steamboat,
Who could be relied on to know each towhead,
Sandbank, sunken wreck, and stump.
I looked up as a knee-high child
Learns to look up for comfort and instruction
And ever after links hope with climbing,
With an office on a higher floor,
With a view from the top of the viewing tower
Where it's easy to meditate in peace and quiet
On the world below, its lack of direction.
Now I'm glad to be strolling along the road
To the stand of maple in Miller's meadow
Where the two of us will unpack our basket.
Come with us if you can concentrate when she's talking
Not only on her words but on the musical hum
Behind them as she stirs the salad.

Try to notice how much of her soul
Inhabits her hands and the line of her cheekbones
And the tilt of her head as she kneels on the cloth,
Her skirt fanned out around her,
A circle on the grass marking the spot

Where sunlight and earth have briefly conjoined.
See how she's glancing your way now
With a look that questions and encourages.
Think of the moment you're afraid to join
As an offering to a god too weak to save us.
What do you think you'll save by holding back?

# Distinctions

The world will be no different if the twin sisters
Disputing now in the linen aisle of Kaufmann's
Resolve their difference about table napkins,
Whether the color chosen by one is violet
Or lavender or washed-out purple. No different,
But that's no reason to deem the talk insignificant.
It's important for people to make distinctions,
To want their words to fit appearances snugly.
Why wait to get home before they decide if the napkins
Match the plates Grandmother gave them years back
For their twentieth birthday? A pleasure to hear them,
Like the pleasure hearing people in a museum
Discuss how closely the landscape approaches
In their experience the best of the Renaissance
Or would if the paint hadn't cracked in spots
And darkened. Should they deem it fine or very fine
Or remarkable? The world no different but the subject
Not insignificant, the whereabouts of the beautiful,
Just how near it lies to the moment
According to a measurement all can agree on.
That was a beautiful conversation last night
About Vermeer though my friend Ramona
Went off on a tangent, hammering home her theory
As to why he never painted his wife or children.
Could be she was feeling resentful she's only third
On her husband's selective roster of the women
Who've left the deepest marks on his character.
But this morning she may be asking herself what right
She has to complain when he's second on hers,
Below the passionate man she walked away from,
Whose curtain lectures on the plight of Cambodia

Bored her silly. No joy for her, back then,
In loving a man whose conscience burdened itself
With the crimes of others, not simply his own.
Now it seems she lost out on a lucky chance
To widen her heart. However painful that thought,
It's useful when she finds herself too satisfied
With the life she has, forgetting where it fits exactly
On the spectrum of ripeness. Meanwhile, out in her garden,
It's a beautiful morning. The air is a little gritty,
Granted, and the clouds gathering in the west
Have lowered its ranking to seven points out of ten
On the scale of likely prospects. But that doesn't mean
She can't make it a ten on the scale of hope,
Ten for her willingness to be proven wrong.

# Land and Sea

Even if we didn't shape it ourselves, the land
Can still serve as our mirror, a grand reminder
Of all we are. Sunrise over the meadow
A sign to light the lamps we already own.
The plowed fields we pass in the car a sign
To bring a part of ourselves under cultivation.
The forests a sign to let some part go wild.
Mountain ranges offer their names to lofty imaginings,
Deserts their names to stretches of arid doubt
When the sweet springs of the soul run dry.
A landscape of linked analogies
That leads us to believe our planet
Has congealed from star ash and cooled
And burgeoned with green with us in mind.
All of it familiar except the greater part,
The ocean, however alive it seems
As it heaves and rolls, a creature
Tossing in its sleep, we want to say,
But under the sway of dreams we can't imagine.
Not likely to be awakened, however loud
The groan of foghorns, however deep
The cut of our prow across its back
As our stout ship plows on towards Tunis or Rome
With a cargo of sandalwood, spices, cotton.
Plows on, we say, anxious for analogies,
But leaving no furrow of soil behind it,
No seeds, no seedlings, no coming harvest.
Now calm, now whipped by the wind into walls
Crashing down on deck, sweeping away the rigging
As a call for help goes out on the radio.
What bearings do we give if we have no landmarks,

Adrift in a region not explored or settled,
Not parceled into counties, not dotted with towns.
The same ocean the earliest sailors saw,
Wine-dark, swayed by the fitful sea gods.
The same implacable enemy to builders and improvers,
Wedging itself between us and the Ithaka
Where lookouts scan the horizon for our sails.

# Grace

The thought of the woman you couldn't make happy
Made happy by someone else
Will have to trouble you less than it does now
If you want to disprove the doctrine of the Fall
And enter the world of grace abounding.

On the day you cross the border, you'll be free.
The town she left won't seem so tiny,
The streets so empty and predictable.
Linger too long with your book at dinner
And you'll miss the walk to the river at dusk
When the rare, shy creatures make their appearance.

Then if you walk away from the town's glare
To watch for a few of the brightest stars,
You won't be doing it to impress her,
To prove you can be intimate with the beautiful
Without a craving for ownership.
You'll be enjoying the stars for their own bright sakes.
There they'll be—Vega, Spica, Aldebaran—
High above the sagging roof of a barn.

On the walk back, you'll linger at the outskirts,
Pausing at an open window to listen.
With the radio waves free of the daytime clutter
Talk shows from Phoenix and Memphis will be coming in clear.
Now they seem a mixture of rancor and confusion.
Then they'll sound like half-truths waiting to be fused
By a power within you still not discovered.

It will be easy then to love the truth
Just for itself, to be content with its cool
Impersonal light. No need to believe
That your contentment, if she learned of it,
Would give her the pleasure she's always wanted.
You'll want to believe she has pleasure enough
Of her own making, should she need to make it,
Should her new friends prove unreliable.
But if they do, you won't be happy. Not then,
When the sweet water of grace begins to flow.

# Consolation

Could be, she tells herself, the Brahmins are right
And she's enjoyed already, in a past existence,
The life that for years she's lamented missing,
Already driven home with her heart's companion,
Who in this existence is driving with someone else.
Already been welcomed by their ducks and dogs
And shared over dinner their plans for tomorrow.
Could be that what tastes to her like longing
Is really memory, the trace not washed from her tongue
When she kneeled to sip the dark water of Lethe.
That's why the house in the country where he lives now
Looked so familiar the one time she dared to pass it,
A weathered farmhouse in the shingle style
Set back from the road in a rising field.
She must have lived there once, a good life,
No doubt about it, selected by her watchful soul,
Who wants the best for her, as this life has been selected,
This climbing the stairs to her city apartment
A block from the discount store, her arms full of groceries.
Already she's planning her project when dinner's done.
This could be the night at her writing desk
When she breaks through the walls of the well-made story
And flows with a loose, associative style
Out to the hollows and crevices of experience.
Her old life won't get her there, to this discovery,
However much she may have learned with her friend
As she read to him on the couch by the stove
Or listened to his reading and commentary.
Does she want to repeat herself, she asks, or move on?
To say she was happier then than now,
To say she's more restless now, and lonely,

Could mean, if the Brahmins are right,
She's stuck in the fiction of the one best life,
Mired in the language of ranking, while the questing soul
Needs many lives to complete its journey,
Each with its own definition of happiness.
The current definition could emerge tonight
As she sits at her desk shaping her thoughts into unity
Long past the hour when her heart's companion
Has gone to bed with his sweetheart to whisper and touch
As once she may have whispered and touched
In a life with him she's promised herself
Not to dwell on now.

# Bivouac Near Trenton

Now that I see my life composed
Of many stories, not one, I needn't worry so much
If I'll be able to see it whole on my deathbed
With any more certainty than I can now.
A relief not to think of it as a war that hinges
On a final battle after years of skirmishes.
Each day reaches its own conclusions by sundown
About the meaning of freedom, its kinship with loyalty.
And if today the armies of General Washington
Had to stage a retreat, Harlem Heights abandoned,
The soldiers who take each day as it comes
Can be happy they didn't panic.
Now they're falling asleep by the river
In tents or in open air, where I'm ready to join them
As soon as I make my devotions to Night,
The goddess who'll protect this day from invasion,
From any plot hatched by tomorrow.
And now as the tent flap rustles in the wind
I'll finish this letter to you by the fitful candle.
It's cold crossing the Delaware in the grip of winter
And at night it's scary, what with the ice floes.
It's warm inside this letter. No need for mittens.
You were out the day the Declaration inspired me
To declare my independence from the tyrant ambivalence,
Who blocked my pursuit of happiness, so I'm writing.
Night has pulled my phrases beyond revision
Up to the safety of the starry sky
Where Jefferson's silvery phrases twinkle untarnished,
Untouched by the story that he died in debt,
Beloved Monticello taken by creditors,
The slaves sold he'd hoped to free.

# Genres

Is it permitted to sit in the shade of the awning
At a roadside cafe and share with strangers
The news of the afternoon and toast the waitress?
Yes, as long as you're sure your story
Is scripted as a comedy where success is identified
With celebrating the moment before it fades.
But not if you're a character on a pilgrimage.
Then you've been tarrying by the way
And won't arrive at the proper turn-off
Just as the slant of the sun renders it visible.
Then your road won't end at the garden
Where you're expected, but at a wall.

Is it permitted, if this is a pilgrimage,
For the pilgrim to hope as he stares at the wall
That he had to act as he did, given his character,
A man unable to grasp how disloyalty
Lurks in an hour's neglect of vigilance
Unless he learns the lesson the hard way.
Yes, if you're sure your story supposes
Character is assigned by the gods.
But what if the actors are allowed to choose
Their outfits of virtue from a full supply room
And you didn't like the drape of courage or stamina?

Is it permitted to consider repentance?
Couldn't a penitent in this story
Be encouraged to retrace his steps,
Taking the long way round past the wall
To the gate of the garden and finally entering?
Yes, if you promise not to be envious

Of those who've arrived decades before you,
People with skills no greater than yours
Who have put them all their lives to higher uses.

But if one can escape the pull of painful comparisons,
Couldn't he be flooded with simple gratitude
He's passed through the gate at last, however late?
Yes, if the thrill of finding it still unlocked
Overcomes the undeniable fact that you've missed
All but the last few scenes before the epilogue,
And the white hair of the man you play is irrelevant
And his stooped shoulders and bent back.

# Two or Three Wishes

Suppose Oedipus never discovers his ignorance
And remains king to the end,
Proud as he walks the streets of Thebes
To think of himself as his city's savior,
The fortunate husband of Queen Jocasta,
The blessed father of two dutiful daughters.
Would we call him happy, a man so unknowing?
If we did, we'd have to admit that happiness
Isn't all we ask for. We want some truth as well,
Whatever that means. We want our notions,
However beautiful and coherent,
Linked to something beyond themselves.
First I want to dream I'm in your thoughts.
Then I want that dream to be a picture
Faithful in flesh and spirit to what is the case.
First I imagine your heart as a city like Thebes
With me as the park you prefer to visit.
Then with my own eyes I want to see you
Resting again and again on one of the benches,
Gathering strength for the messenger
Who may be nearing the outskirts now
Wondering if you'll know how to take the news.

# Integer

Shall I give up on salvation
And suppose the unit of life isn't the self,
As I've always assumed, but the twenty houses
That make up my block? Which house puts in the hours
Required each month by the block's one conscience
Won't be the issue then, as long as the slot gets filled.
A comfort then to wake before dawn
And glimpse through curtains the light
Already burning in my neighbor's study,
Proof that the block's quota of early writing
Is on its way to completion and I can sleep in
Or drive to the farmer's market for groceries
Since shopping too is a category of useful action
And spaces are still blank on the sign-up sheet.
No need to be first, no need to enlarge
The margin of experience beyond what's given.
A life without emulation; a death that's calm
As I accept the end of my many projects
And my dream of heaven. The street
Will survive me. My dust will return to it,
And my soul, too, though smaller than I imagined,
No bigger than a katydid in a bush by a gate
As it helps a yard meet its quota of squeaking.

# Writing at Night

This empty feeling that makes me fearful
I'll disappear the minute I stop thinking
May only mean that beyond the kitchen window, in the dark,
The minions of the past are gathering,
Waiting for the dishes to be cleared away
So they can hustle supper into oblivion.

This feeling may only mean that supper's done
And night has the house surrounded
And the past is declaring itself the victor.
It doesn't deny that tomorrow I'll wake to find
That the usual bales of light have been unloaded
And distributed equally in every precinct,
That the tree at the corner is awash in it
And the flaming, yellow coats of the crossing guards.

This empty feeling could be a gift
I haven't yet grown used to, a lightness
That means I've shaken off the weight of resentment,
Envy, remorse, and pride that drags the soul down.
A thinness that lets me slip through a needle's eye
Into the here and now of the kitchen
Without losing a button.

An emptiness that betokens a talent for self-forgetting
That lets me welcome the stories of others,
Which even now may be on their way,
Hoping I'll take them in however rumpled they look
And gray-faced as they drag themselves from the car

With their bulky night bags and water jugs.
It's late. Have I gone to bed? they wonder.
And then they see the light in the kitchen
And a figure who could be me at the table
Still up writing.

# Still Life

Now's a good time, before the night comes on,
To praise the loyalty of the vase of flowers
Gracing the parlor table, and the bowl of oranges,
And the book with freckled pages resting on the tablecloth.
To remark how these items aren't conspiring
To pack their bags and move to a place
Where stillness appears to more advantage.
No plan for a heaven above, beyond, or within,
Whose ever-blooming bushes are rustling
In a sea breeze at this very moment.
These things are focusing all their attention
On holding fast as time washes around them.
The flowers in the vase won't come again.
The page of the book beside it, the edge turned down,
Will never be read again for the first time.
The light from the window's angled.
The sun's moving on. That's why the people
Who live in the house are missing.
They're all outside enjoying the light that's left them.
Lucky for them to find when they return
These silent things just as they were.
Night's coming on and they haven't been frightened off.
They haven't once dreamed of going anywhere.

# Starry Night

Only a few stars are visible when I step outside
For a walk to the mailbox with my packet of poems.
In a week or two Mary will take time out
From preparing her class on Melville
To mark the lines that seem to need more work.
If I don't agree with her now, it's likely I will
In a month or two when I gain more distance.
Are other writers as lucky in their friends as I am
Or do they go it alone, as Melville did?
To get some distance on *Billy Budd*, he left the manuscript
Untouched for six months in the dark of a desk drawer,
The last six months of his life, it turned out.
Maybe he was planning to go back to it
For a final review and then search for a publisher
If publishing still mattered to him
And he thought a story so far from the fashion
For middling characters could find a public.
A book so different from the one I'm writing,
The way it reveals its truth in extremes.
How boldly Melville likens his sailor hero
To Adam before the Fall and then to Jesus.
On the lid of the box that held the papers
He pasted the words, "Be true to the dreams of thy youth."
And if he felt true, as is likely, what more did he need?
Here is the mailbox, and this is the comforting sound
Of my packet of poems hitting the bottom.
And now it's time to walk back under the streetlights,
Wondering what a youthful dream of adventure
Would conclude if it could see me,

How much explaining it would ask me for
And how much revision, if it thought revision
One of the choices still available.

# Your City

How much would it take for this city
That so far has belonged to others
To be yours as well,
The houses set in rows and each row named
So you can find the garden of your new acquaintance
Long before sundown, just as you promised,
And the talk has time to wander and pause.

How much as you walk home in the dark
For the portly policeman, who now
Stands on the corner for others,
To stand for you by the grocery store
Still open for your convenience,
The lettuce and cucumber planted last spring
For you as well, weeded and watered,
Picked this very week, sorted and loaded,
And driven along a highway where a highway crew
Has worked all month for you digging a culvert.

How much for the book on the nightstand at home,
Written now for others, to be written for you
In hours stolen from sleep and children,
Sweet and bitter wisdom distilled as a gift
As the author guesses you're coming along
In need of encouragement and of warning.

Three weeks till it's due at the local library.
How much would it take for the right
To wander the stacks all afternoon,
Wrested for others from kings and shamans,
To be wrested for you as well,

And the Constitution amended to protect your rights
Against the privileges of the few
And the prejudice of the many.

You learned the story in school but couldn't believe it.
How much would it take for it all to be possible,
To walk the streets of a glimmering city
Begemmed with houses of worship and lecture halls
That thrust the keys to bliss into your hands.
A city where for you as well
Mohammed decides to linger at Mecca
And Jesus rides his donkey into crazed Jerusalem
And Moses descends the mountain and loving Buddha
Turns his back on heaven, hearing your sighs.

How long a wait till invisible hands,
That have left instructions for others
In every lonely hotel room, lead you
To lock up evil and coax the good
From whatever corner of your soul it's fled to,
The beleaguered good you've always imagined
Looking for others to deliver it
When all along it's looked for you.

# About the Author

Carl Dennis lives in Buffalo, where he teaches literature and creative writing at the State University of New York. He also serves on the faculty of the nonresidency M.A. Program in Creative Writing at Warren Wilson College. A recipient of a Guggenheim Fellowship and a grant from the National Foundation of the Arts, he has published six other books of poetry, most recently *The Outskirts of Troy* and *Meetings with Time*.